just so you know

COMPILED BY PAMELA A. STOVALL
PHOTOGRAPHY BY KAREN BOURDIER

Printed and bound in Canada by Art Bookbindery

www.ArtBookbindery.com

ISBN 978-0-9768335-1-2

Introduction

As a young teenager I had a neighbor who I really admired. The thing I observed most was how she disciplined her three children. She was firm, no nonsense, but very loving. I decided right then that she was who I wanted to emulate in that area. That woman was just one of innumerable women who have impacted my life to help me develop into the woman I am today. I watched and learned. I listened and deciphered. I took the good and set aside the bad. That is the function of a role model, and that is what this book is all about.

Young women, you need us! You need us to teach you and help you learn from our mistakes – not because we think we know it all, but because we love you enough to want to make it a little easier for you. They say "Experience is the best teacher," but I say, "Why have a bad experience if you can learn from someone else's?"

Titus 2: 3-4 states, "Similarly, teach the older women to live in a way that is appropriate for someone serving the Lord. …they should teach others what is good. These older women must train the younger women to love their husbands and their children, to live wisely and be pure…" (NLT).

All the contributors to this book have taken to heart Paul's admonition to teach the younger women. We want you to know yourselves better than we knew ourselves at your age. We want you to be more successful than we were. We want you to be powerful women of God who will lead your generation on a straight path. We pray that the wisdom found in this book will spice up your life and help you find your way to a prosperous, peace-filled, successful life with God at the helm, always.

Through a Mirror Dimly

Now that I am older, I realize I wasted a lot of years despising the one I saw in the mirror. I judged her and compared her to others. I always compared her weaknesses to the strengths of others.

I saw her through her mistakes, failures and the rejection she experienced from other people. I rejected her because of her imperfections and weakness. I never allowed her to just be who she was without always pointing out her wrongs. I called her stupid for loving men who treated her badly. In my eyes she was never pretty enough, small enough, smart enough or good enough, no matter how hard she tried.

Then one day, I met a man who told me He loved her in spite of her imperfections. It was then I realized that if He could love and accept her, then perhaps *I* was too hard on her.

This man continued to love her unconditionally, and now, I no longer hate the one I saw in the mirror. I began to see her through this Man's eyes. I realize I was wrong about her all the time.

God showed me how to embrace, accept and love myself just as I am.

Thira Simon

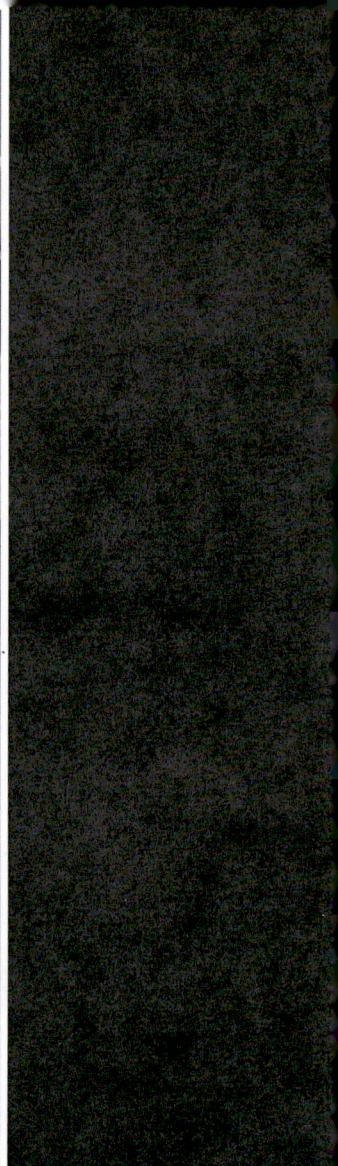

Tenacious!

In 2008, my brother Kenny and I lost the most precious thing in our lives: Mother. Never could I have imagined the pain of losing one's mother. Mother was physically and spiritually beautiful and vivacious; her smile could light up any room. She possessed a photographic memory and would give her family the shirt off her back.

When we were 5 and 6, Mother worked for $15 per week at a laundry. She had the courage to take the Postal Service Clerk's test. To pass this test, you had to know where every city's mail in the state was delivered. She studied with hundreds of white cards with cities and/or zip codes in Georgia on them. I recall that she did not pass this test at least twice. It had to be nerves because, as previously stated, she had a photographic memory. She would cry so heart-wrenchingly at her failure. We would pat her on the back giving her encouragement. Soon afterwards, she would dry her tears and start studying again. Maybe it was the third time that she passed the test.

Our lives changed drastically! We weren't middle class by any means when she went to work for the government but from where we started, it felt like we were rich. How Mother handled this situation taught me a great life lesson: never give up, always have a positive attitude; and when you fall down, pick yourself up, get back in the race and work harder than anybody else.

This was my first lesson developing a strong work ethic. I've discovered that I am not the brightest nor the swiftest at grasping tasks, often appearing clumsy at first; but I can be the most tenacious and will give my all every time. This strong work ethic, I owe to my beloved Mother, Anna.

Pat Avery

Joy's Medicine

One of the most valuable lessons that God has taught me in 50 years of living has, surprisingly, come while journeying down the rockiest of roads. God has shown me the reality that even in the midst of hardship, He will strengthen me as I purposefully choose an attitude of joy!

Even though the terms "happiness" and "joy" are used interchangeably, they are actually a reverse of each other. We experience happiness when circumstances are good, but joy is given only by trusting in the Lord in times when circumstances are anything but good. Joy is a precious gift given to us by God as He reminds us that He is with us in every situation. As a follower of Jesus, I find joy in knowing that His love is unconditional, that He understands all that I face, and that He will provide for my needs. Joy does not depend on what I am experiencing but is found in the promises and steadfastness of Jesus.

If I had only realized much earlier in life the power that comes from living with an attitude of choosing joy, rather than facing difficulties with despair, I would have experienced the strength that God supplies when I look to Him to provide. Proverbs 17:22 tells us that "A joyful heart is good medicine, but a broken spirit dries up the bones."

There was a particular period in my life when I faced an intense ongoing emotional pain. During that time, as I cried out to the Lord for His help, I experienced a joy that I could never have manufactured in my own power. "The joy of the Lord is your strength." (Nehemiah 8:10)

I've learned that difficult times are inevitable to everyone, but God can give me the strength to make it through those times and to become stronger having gone through them.

Shari Griffin

Temple Maintenance

I was kind of weird as a kid, but not necessarily in a bad way. Strangely enough, I was one who actually loved fruits and vegetables. Seriously! All the other kids around me, including my siblings enjoyed the usual teenage fare: fast food, chips, soda, etc. Don't get me wrong, I liked candy, ice cream and other junk food occasionally, but I mostly took great pleasure in non-traditional foods for someone my age, like broccoli and cabbage and salad and fresh fruit.

We had an open campus, so we were allowed to go out for lunch if we wanted. While my classmates darted for the closest sub shop or pizza place, I often found myself hunting for a produce market. One store, in particular, sold the largest, most succulent apples you ever tasted. That is what I wanted most.

I was also very athletic. When the other girls were making excuses to get out of P.E., I couldn't wait to get into the gym. I loved being challenged in gymnastics and other sports. I enjoyed the competition.

I miss those times. Somehow, as I have gotten older, I have become rather lazy about good nutrition and exercise. Not really sure why, but boy, oh boy, do I regret it! Now, I have health issues that I'm certain can be corrected, or, at the very least, improved with a healthier diet and more consistent exercise. Would that I'd had the wisdom to appreciate what I had then – enough to hold onto it for dear life!

God's Word tells us that our bodies are His temple. Therefore, we are obligated to take good care of them. I'm learning to appreciate what God has given me so that I can remain strong long enough to fulfill what He has called me to do. It's a struggle, but I'm on my way.

Pamela A. Stovall

Roots and Wings

Although we too often take it for granted, being part of a family involves one of the deepest needs in mankind - the need to belong, the need to be accepted unconditionally "just because." Just because we are born into families physically, we belong. Whether we are brought into families by birth, marriage, or adoption, family is where we get our first impressions of life, and it is usually with family that we take our last breath on earth.

God uses family words to identify himself. He is the Father, Jesus the Son, Mary is the mother through whom Jesus came.

Families were created before the church. They give us roots and wings; they test us and help form our character. Family is present at all the significant social events of our life: our birthdays, graduations, marriage, and children's births. Family is our first school. Here we learn good and bad habits. Twelve step groups help us take inventory of what we learned in early family life as well as later. They teach us to keep what is healthy and ask God to remove what is unhealthy or toxic such as blame and resentments.

Home is where the heart is. "Going home" symbolizes acceptance and safety. It is the reward after a long journey, a sickness or mental warfare. The matriarch and patriarch (or one or the other) usually keeps the family together. They take the family on trips or have family dinners or outdoor barbecues or have family meetings to solve problems or celebrate events. Visits to grandparents, great grandparents, aunts, uncles, etc. help keep families close. Of course, going to church together and praying for one another is a great way to keep families together. As the old adage says, "Families that pray together stay together."

Whatever it takes, stay connected; that is the key. Stay connected to God and to one another. We have strong roots and fruitful "wings" and can encourage these in our children.

Joy Crenshaw

Cab Money in My Shoe

Being open about my dating experience and what I wish I had known is definitely on my agenda. I cannot go back and relive those years, but I certainly can prepare my children.

I grew up in a very trusting environment where I had a strong sense of security, despite the typical family problems that we all face. My mother was in sales and my father worked in construction, so I saw them interact with different types of people all the time. This made me very comfortable and trusting with just about anyone.

I spent a lot of time with people from church. My preconceptions were crushed on my first date with the son of a church deacon. Looking back, I wish I had done some research on how to ward off a charging octopus in the wild. His hands were EVERYWHERE!!! At home that night, I sat stunned and wondered how such a prodigal was spawned by a man I had looked up to for a very long time.

The next chapter of my life was on the campus of a prominent Christian university. I thought that I was in Beulah land, surrounded by young people who were just as zealous about their faith as I was. My anticipation of dating godly young men fizzled fast when my date had all the moves of a Gatling gun. I was exhausted within 30 minutes and never went on a date again without cab money in my shoe.

Some of the young men I encountered were honorable, but that did not mean that they were not vulnerable. Girls are much better at demanding honor; and when they do, the good guys will rise to the occasion.

Beth Middleton

A New Me Everyday

I mulled over this letter to my "younger self" for many days. The wisdom I have to share centers around one thing – love – love of self, love of family, and love of God.

First, self --- Like many young girls, I had a big heart and was more beautiful than I ever perceived myself to be. If only I had the self confidence that I have now, boy, would I be a force to reckoned with! I found ways of supporting my weaknesses by surrounding myself with people who exemplified the things I wanted for myself. This was a good thing because each of these people taught me something. That is one of the smartest things I ever did. I learned to love myself as I am at each moment. I am not the same person today that I was a year ago or will be a year from now. So I get to love a new me everyday!

Second, family --- With every joy comes some pain. Every one of my greatest memories and warm, fuzzy feelings came with some price. The love of my husband, Robert, is a wonderful gift, but it is work everyday to make what we have precious. Our four rug rats and loves of my life, Chelsea, Kyle, Reece and Jessica, each came with their own labor. We've learned in our family that it is ok to disagree. We can all still live, love and work together and not always agree on the same things.

Last, but most importantly, God --- Loving God requires a relationship with Him and relationship requires some talking. I talk to God everyday – riding in the car, walking up stairs, doing laundry, or combing my daughter's hair. God is the best friend I will ever have. He's a great listener, too. I ask him for anything and oh, how bountifully he gives to me!

Mary Ann Reid

Sweeter and Deeper

At the church I attended growing up, each week's birthdays, anniversaries and spiritual birthdays were celebrated at a general gathering during Sunday School. Celebrants paid a penny for each year they were celebrating and were serenaded with the appropriate song depending on the occasion. Many of the older women would often describe their relationships with God as getting sweeter and deeper when they testified while paying for their spiritual birthdays. Never discussed was the cost. Sweeter and deeper comes with a price.

A growing and developing relationship with God requires constant cultivation. Each time the relationship grows, God asks for (and requires) more. Sometimes God repackages dreams and plans to strategically conform them to his will. Many times, drawing closer requires a test where trusting God is the only answer. The reward for drawing closer to God is an abiding peace and assurance.

When I realize the higher cost for my relationship with God, I rest in the confidence of knowing I am his child. He's a loving parent aware of what He has planned for my life. I'm not always aware of the plan and have to walk by faith, trusting Him to take me where he needs me.

In those times, I've learned to take to heart truth that brings light and encouragement to my soul in my darkest hours. At the foundation of my relationship with God is Psalm 27, which I rely on when I need comfort, consolation, encouragement, protection, peace … anything. I've found verse 14 to usually have the most relevance: "Wait for the Lord; be strong and take heart and wait for the Lord."

A growing and developing relationship with God requires courage and waiting – courage to face the test coming to make the relationship stronger and waiting to understand why God sent the test and how it configures in his plan. While the price is steep, the reward is well worth the cost.

Karen L. Bates

Caught in Mid Air!

Purity brings to mind the feel of a cool morning breeze, the freshness of a summer rain or the innocence of a child's face. In our minds we know the look, feel and even the taste of purity. When you see it, you recognize it, want it, even strive for it…. only to be reminded of its illusiveness.

As intelligent consumers, we desire the purest water to quench our thirst. Our actions are very deliberate to obtain the level of goodness we desire. This tight rope we walk to obtain this purity is high, and the fall is unforgiving. Fear whispers in our ear, reminding us that we will certainly lose our footing.

Purity cannot be obtained, so we ask ourselves, "Why even try?" Our hearts quickly remind us (and sometimes our emotions reveal) the frustration in this contradiction. What I want to do, I cannot achieve. The purity I desire seems unattainable. Personal discipline, influence or money cannot obtain what my very being longs for. Lower my expectations (lower the tightrope) and the fall hurts far less. Time and humanness guarantee that I will topple, which to some degree, soon occurs.

Bracing for the fall and ready for the impact, there is no time or interest in excuses or explanations. "Help!" is the word that conveys my desperation. Hope answers my call. The safety net of God's grace catches me in mid air. I knew it was there from the beginning but had not planned on needing it. Grace captures me as I awkwardly attempt to regain my composure. God's love and grace remind me that He alone is pure. Faith speaks to my fears, and trust follows. With joy and relief, I admit that *I* cannot obtain this purity, but love propels me to try again.

Linda Combs Sculley

Backlashes and Cold Shoulders

When I was a child, my mother was always there. I loved her. I can truly say I appreciated her. But she didn't seem like a separate person, a person with her own feelings. She was "Mom." She was always there.

As I grew, I came to realize that my mother was indeed a person with her own (very real) feelings. And after I had my own daughters, I understood what it was like to be a mother.

I understood what it was like to feel complete, unalterable love for another human being. I understood that it wasn't that my mother lacked feelings when I was a child – she just put my feelings ahead of her own. She rejoiced with me when I scored the winning run in a pivotal softball game. She cried with me when no one asked me to the prom; and when she punished me, it wasn't because she was evil (something of which I was convinced at the time).

I now understand that my punishments were tougher on my mother than they were on me. It would have been so much easier to let me get away with my transgressions. But she chose to take the harder path because it helped me learn to become a better person. I realize now that when my mother took the time and energy to set me straight, and endure my backlashes and cold shoulders, was actually when she loved me most.

Your mother will rejoice in your happiness – cherish her.
Your mother will feel your pain when you're sad – embrace her.
Your mother will make mistakes – forgive her.
You and your mother will disagree – respect her, even if you don't agree with her.
And know that when your mother is the toughest on you, when she refuses to let you accept less than your best, is when she loves you most.

Anonymous

Radiant Modesty

One of the ways we sometimes try to reflect our personalities and how we feel is by the way we dress. A special occasion usually warrants a desire to dress more feminine, being seen by others in a different light than we're seen during normal days. But the impression we leave with others is one that will remain in their minds long after the occasion has passed. It's up to each of us to consider the long-term image that we leave with others in the way we are seen.

This same thought holds true in the way we dress in everyday settings. First impressions are normally lasting ones. Whether it's showing up for a job interview, meeting new friends or family members, making a business or social call - opinions are formed about us as soon as others see us, so it's good to think about that as we prepare for the day. This is not to say that our clothing must be expensive, nor does it need to be new. However, it should be fitting for the occasion.

1 Timothy 2:9-10 states, "I also want women to dress modestly, with decency and propriety, not with braided hair or gold or pearls or expensive clothes, but with good deeds, appropriate for women who profess to worship God." (NIV)

This scripture is not to be interpreted as, "Dressing up isn't suitable," but rather it focuses on modesty and the manner in which we act and how we treat others around us. It's often said that a true Christian doesn't have to go around talking about being one, but rather the spirit within us will radiate through the ways we act, things we say and what we do. Looks change, but memories of the way we act hold steadfast in the minds of others.

Verna Rutherford

Who Validates Your Ticket?

I imagined that I went back into the past to speak to my former self. After I convinced her that *I* was her, this is what I said:

Although life is very satisfying in the future, I want you to enjoy your life so much more now. I'll give you the secret. If you listen to me, you will look at yourself more positively and avoid making the painful mistakes that will leave you feeling guilty and condemned.

Look at yourself through God's eyes, and not man's. Psalms 139:14 says, "I praise you because I am fearfully and wonderfully made: Your works are wonderful." I know people are making fun of you and you wish you looked different, but rejecting yourself is like rejecting the God who made you. You will grow up to be a confident woman, who is not only beautiful on the outside but even more beautiful on the inside.

Put your confidence in God, not man. In Psalms 56:4, David writes, "…in God I put my confidence: I will not fear; what can man do to me?" (NIV) You are so afraid to be yourself because of what the kids at school might say. You shouldn't care about their opinions of you. What can they do to you? Nothing! Be who you are in Christ and don't let peer pressure turn you into something you are not.

Finally, you don't need validation from boys or men. This is probably the most important piece of advice I could give you. Write this down and keep it close to your heart. Get your validation from God. He is the only One who will tell you the truth because He loves you. There is no "Knight in Shining Armor." Psalms 118:9 says, "It is better to take refuge in the Lord, than to trust in princes." (NIV)

Trust me, you will be fine, but let's start *now.*

Ivy A. Stegall

IOU Love

When I graduated from college, I was so excited to finally have my own income and all the freedom that came along with it. With that "freedom" came a credit card with a generous spending limit. So I started spending and spending and spending. I eventually ran up debt. Then I lost my job! And the excitement I once felt quickly turned into fear. I not only had credit card debt, I had a car payment and a student loan. What was I going to do?

I had to decide right then and there who my provider was. Was it a job that, quite frankly, I never really liked? Or was it my parents, to whom I could always run? Or was I going to let God show Himself faithful and truly be my provider—the source of all that I needed?

I learned very quickly that God *is* my provider. He supplies resources to meet my needs—a job, family, etc., but ultimately, He is the SOURCE! And it's to Him that I must turn for everything I need.

I also learned what true financial freedom is. Romans 13:8 says, "Don't run up debts, except for the huge debt of love you owe each other" (The Message). True financial freedom is to be debt free.

April K. Tyler

Who "Made" the List?

I am so blessed to have an incredible husband. We are ridiculously in love and very active in making our marriage a peaceful, joy-filled and safe, covenant relationship.

Finding my soul mate was not easy. I learned over time that I only thought I knew what my needs were going to be in a husband. See, God knows us better than we know ourselves. He knows our weaknesses, strengths, and who we will need for accountability and balance. His will is better than our own.

When I was dating, I wrote down a list of silly things that I wanted in a husband and I was swept off my feet by someone who met every detail on "the list." The relationship turned out to be a stumbling block in my relationship with the Lord and my parents and altered my personality. I changed the way I walked, talked and dressed, and none of these in a positive way. It was shocking to me that even though he made "the list," this person was nothing I needed in a partner. God slammed the door shut on that relationship. I see him today and thank God for giving me the ability to pray His will for my life. His mercy is the only reason I am walking in my destiny today, and my husband is huge part of that.

The most important part in finding a spouse is asking God to be a part of the process. Too many make the mistake of not involving the Lord and then they want Him to clean up the mess of a marriage they have made. Allowing God to take control of that part of your life may seem illogical; but trust me, faith in God is the most logical thing we can do.

Pastor Lindsay Clark

Tarnished to Polished

"Beauty lies in the eyes of the beholder." What an overused statement that is so often made without understanding of the true meaning behind those simple words! I am reminded of this as I stumble across an old tattered and worn necklace with tarnished beads thrown off to the side of a cluttered table at a garage sale, where much of the merchandise would be labeled as "junk" by most passers-by. I pick it up, looking not at what it is, but at what it can be. For, I know the true meaning of the word "beauty."

You see, I spent much of my time feeling pushed off to the side watching life pass me by. I was not beautiful or popular and thought that my constant struggle with weight would define me for the rest of my life. BUT, somewhere along my life's journey, I realized that I had the power, hidden deep down inside of me, to change the direction of the path I was wandering down, and that I could no longer allow myself to drown in the sea of ugliness and uselessness that I had been shoved under as a child.

In my mid-twenties, I made the conscious decision to intentionally re-invent myself and break through any barrier that was placed in front of me. I was no longer going to allow myself to be overlooked, like some tattered piece of jewelry; but instead, I was going to allow my true beauty to shine through, from the inside out. Twenty-five years later, I can now say that I have no boundaries.

As I transform this old necklace, placing each freshly polished bead on a new, strong wire, I am reminded of each obstacle that I have faced and overcome throughout my life. I now can look back knowing that these hurdles were all necessary phases of life which have molded me into the woman I am today.

Carolyn Pineda

Waiting Well

I didn't learn much about life planning and waiting well as a young woman. A major life crisis taught me how to wait and what to do while waiting.

It wasn't easy removing my first wedding band. Symbolically my life was as vulnerable as my bare fingers. A pale band remained where the custom-made ring had been. I had it melted down and remolded into a dinner ring. My heart melted too. Tears were just below the surface. The lump in my throat remained swollen. I so desired to have a sense of power over anything in my messed-up life.

I liked being married, being a wife, being a mother. *Surely there would be another husband for me,* I thought. No one came along. So I waited. I'd often watch with envy as others dated and sometimes remarried. At the ballpark I cheered alongside moms and dads who went off to home together. Going out was terribly awkward. No man seemed to be a match. So – I waited.

While I waited I decided to become more the person I was capable of being. I went back to college for a master's degree. All of my skills were challenged in the process. I gained much more than a degree. My self confidence soared. My children had new adventures. My salary increased. Eventually I became a more appealing woman for men that interested me. By being my best self, I attracted dates with men who were also functioning at their best.

After dating Sam for about four years, he gave me a spectacular engagement ring. I took it to show my daughter who knew about diamonds. She examined it, carefully counting the pavé diamonds under the solitaire. She said, "Mom, there are sixteen—one for every year you waited."

"Never view waiting as wasted time, these are simply opportune moments allotted for the purpose of regaining some inner stillness, calm and clarity." -Michele Howe

Gail Cawley Showalter

Wastrel or Steward?

My thoughts were centered on the immediate future. What would I wear? Where would I go on the weekend? How could I handle my obligations (school) and still do what I wanted to do? I could buy books and never read them, subscribe to magazines and throw them in the trash, wash dishes and let the water run continuously, and take long, long showers. Never once did I consider how I was wasting the resources God provided. My view changed drastically with age!

My dad owned a sawmill and thought nothing of clear cutting the trees. Although I worked at his office, I thought nothing of it either. We thought it strange that people wanted to preserve the Big Thicket. Now I am part of that group, an avid recycler and wish I had been involved at a younger age. Being a wastrel, (a wasteful person), is one thing we do not want to be. We can do simple things like planting a tree, using canvas shopping bags instead of plastic, donating clothes, furniture, books, magazines, computer equipment, cell phones, and ink cartridges, and planting a garden (herbs and/or vegetables) in our yard or in containers. We must strive to leave the world a healthier place than we found it.

If only I had stopped to think how important caring for God's earth was then. "The Lord God took the man and put him in the garden of Eden to till it and keep it." (Genesis 2:15 RSV) Now I know how important it is today. As a result of this revelation, I have tried to teach my grandchildren about recycling and conservation. At a younger age, we must think about how our actions will affect our future.

Elaine Allums

Give it Back, Thief!

As a young woman, I was clueless about the real meaning and power of the Gospel of Jesus Christ. I attended church regularly with my loving family, but as too many Christians do, I subscribed to a "no fault" religion. If anything bad happened or if I experienced failure or defeat, I chalked it up to part of God's mysterious plan for my life. I imagined that He must be trying to teach me something and it would end up being a proverbial "blessing in disguise" anyway. Oh, how wrong I was!

Praise the Lord that He has taught me through His Word that Christ bore our poverty, sins, sicknesses, and diseases at Calvary so that we could be redeemed and blessed with health, salvation, and prosperity. It is Satan who comes to steal, kill, and destroy, but Christ has come that we may have and enjoy an abundant, full life.

My husband and I had been blessed with a happy marriage and successful legal careers, but we had no children. We went through many unpleasant (and expensive) medical treatments to no avail. Unfortunately, at that time we did not know a very important truth: Christ had redeemed us from all sickness and disease, including infertility. I regret that I accepted infertility as His will for my life when it was not. However, in His mercy and compassion, God blessed my husband and me with a beautiful baby girl, whom we adopted as an infant and adore.

Today, my husband and I know the Good News of the Gospel of Jesus Christ and what He purchased for us. By faith, we walk in the fullness of the blessing of Jesus Christ and we assert our authority as born-again believers of His redemptive work and power. We have seized on the living, breathing Word of God and will never let go!

Cherie H. Gall

Get Up and Read!

"Hate me now, love me later." Those were my mother's favorite words. She would say them after coming into our room around 7:00 am, on a Saturday morning, in the summertime, banging on the wall and telling us it was time to get up! "You can't sleep all day; get up and read. Read something. I don't care what you read, a comic book, a magazine, the newspaper, the cookbook; it doesn't matter as long as you read." We knew the drill, "The more you read, the more you know, and a good education is something no one can take away from you."

After going away to college, I would call crying to come home; but my mom would say no. She would always tell me, "Dry them up (my tears); everything will be all right. Learn everything that you can, and it will pay off." I didn't think the woman loved me anymore as she was determined that I was going to complete school. I don't know how she did it, but there were three of us in college at the same time. For my generation, it was a privilege to be able to go to college.

I didn't understand it then, but I eventually figured it out. There are endless possibilities in what you can do with a good foundation and education. I never dreamed what I could be as a kid who started out at the age of 14, participating in a summer youth program for economically disadvantaged youth. I now head that organization that gave me that first job. God's word says, "My people are destroyed for lack of knowledge." (Hosea 4:6a, KJV). You can always keep learning; don't ever stop. Lean on God for your strength and forge ahead, even in the tough times.

Marilyn Smith

A Cushy Life

Stress! Whether mother, daughter, newlywed, or single gal, we all have to deal with it. My family and coworkers could quickly tell you my most frequent symptoms of stress - anxiety, irritability, and agitation. I feel the heat from time pressure for getting multiple things done, from unexpected problems that arise, and from concerns about family members.

Through the years I've experimented with various ways of dealing with stress – music, humor, exercise, deep breathing, rest, prayer, vitamins, and cushions. Ah ha! I bet you didn't expect to see cushions in the list. Sofa cushions? No, although a relaxing evening on the sofa can often help. Time cushions and financial cushions are the stress softeners for me.

When I just HAVE to be somewhere at a certain time, I leave in time to be there at least 10 minutes early. When I have a deadline to meet, I schedule so as to finish a fair amount of time sooner than the deadline. Before I go to bed at night, I make sure everything I'll need for getting ready the next morning is all laid out – keys, purse, glasses, charged cell phone, and ironed clothes. This provides a welcome time cushion the next morning since I'm often sleepy-headed then.

I've been very fortunate to have been a saver from days as a small child, putting my pennies and nickels away in a plastic golden egg bank. Not only has this habit saved money through the years, it has cushioned me from financial stress when unexpected expenses arise. Living below my means and minimal dependence on credit have been two cornerstones to creating this financial cushion.

These cushions are not so much stress relievers as they are stress preventers. Here's to a cushy life!

Karen Bourdier

Humbly in Charge

Very early in my career, when I was in my early twenties I was elevated to a position of authority, asked to lead women – peers – with more experience and seniority than me. I quickly learned that there's a difference between being a leader and just being in charge.

What sets a leader apart from a mere boss is that she sets an example for those around her. Leading by example requires you to evaluate what you're doing, why you're doing it, and how it will be perceived. It means expecting a lot from yourself before demanding it of others, and objectively evaluating your own performance to ensure that you are meeting and exceeding the standards you've set for those around you. Leading by example means recognizing good advice when you hear it, and following through on good ideas that aren't your own. Someone else's innovation shouldn't be a challenge to your authority, but rather an opportunity for success, and a chance to nurture another potential leader. Leading by example means showing self-control when you're frustrated. Doing otherwise is tacit approval for those around you to be less than gracious. In short, leading by example means having a good handle on your self-image.

A strong self-image does not mean blind self-confidence, but rather the confidence to accept that you have made mistakes and will make mistakes again, hold yourself accountable, learn and move on. As a business leader in my community, and as the Mayor of my city, Beaumont, Texas, the lessons I learned about leadership as I started my career are some of the most valuable I've learned, and they are still with me today.

Mayor Becky Ames

Drop the Mask!

Titus 2:4-5: "These older women must train the younger women to love their husbands and their children, to live wisely and be pure, to work in their homes, to do good and to be submissive to their husbands. Then they will not bring shame on the word of God." (NLBT)

Children, children, children everywhere! All of a sudden we had three children of our own, and we had become foster parents to teenage girls – girls who had been mistreated and neglected in their own homes. We were a church-going family at this time, and I was a Sunday School teacher.

When the teaching on Sunday didn't line up with what was happening on *Tuesday* in our home, I was made painfully aware of it by the girls. I began to realize that these very troubled young girls wanted absolute honesty. If what was being taught was not practiced at home, they rebelled. It was just another dishonest lifestyle - and they instinctively knew they wanted better.

That's been 35 plus years ago, but it was good training for ministry. If the Word of God is not alive in us, most especially in our home life, it will not bring LIFE to those who reside there. Life begets life. Because of the need to be totally transparent to our own children, as well as "hurting" young girls, I learned that what I was ministering, whether by music or by verbal communication, had to be LIFE to me to beget LIFE in other people.

The best product you will ever produce is to be the kind of mother who is totally transparent and honest with what you believe and do in your own home behind closed doors. Always remember, the anointing of God will take you places you never dreamed of, but you'll only stay there if your character is intact.

Sharon Benell

Shine, Baby, Shine!

When thinking about starting your career, be mindful of several things. This is your time to shine! You have already laid the groundwork by preparing yourself educationally; now it's time to present yourself as knowledgeable and skilled.

Be sure to prepare a professional, exciting resume. Then practice interviewing skills. Although it may be difficult to "brag" about yourself, you will have to for the potential employer to know what you can do! He needs to know how you stand out among the crowd, but be careful not to come across as arrogant. Tell about yourself and list your proficiencies and abilities. Talk about what organizations you joined and what roles you played in the organizations.

Okay, let's say you've done all the right things, had a killer resume, gave an impressive interview, and landed the job of your dreams. What's next? How do you proceed to the next step – actually doing the job?

Prepare yourself to be the "new" employee. Don't be afraid; but remember, as you did during the interview, there is a thin line between arrogance and humility. Ride the line well. Don't go into the job and brag about what you have earned and what you know. Yes, you are proud of it, but remember to never diminish the accomplishments of your fellow employees. Open your mind to learn from seasoned colleagues.

Open your mind to be a great example – not one to gossip, lag, whine, etc. Take out the negative and inhale the positive aspects, and make it into what you need it to be for your job path. Expect to do your best, to learn something new, and expect God to show up in your life each workday to grow you into a great employee.

Stay prayerful. Good luck, keep in touch, and keep God first in your life and He will direct all of your paths.

Yolanda Avery

Gentle Plucking

When we're young, very rarely do we think about the kind of parents we might be. Most of us know whether we want children or not, and we might even make the decision not to do certain things the way our parents did. Now that I'm older, I realize how challenging raising a child is.

Parenting, in many ways, is like tending a garden. I can't have beautiful flowers without watering them and keeping the weeds out. If I plant flowers and do not take any time to care for or maintain them, the flowers will grow up, but their beauty will be crowded out by weeds. Just as flowers need a gardener's time and care, my daughter needed me to plant the word of God in her heart in order to prevent weeds (unrighteousness) from growing in there. With much prayer, insight, and wisdom from God, I watched over my child, wisely plucking out the weeds of her life in gentle ways, being careful not to provoke wrath and rebellion.

God instructs parents in Deuteronomy 6:4-9 to be committed to telling our children about Him and instructing them in love for God and God's way (righteousness.) "Talk about them when you sit at home and when you walk along the road, when you lie down and when you get up." (NIV) I quickly learned that this was my parental duty, and it should not be left up to the Church as a lesson just for Sundays.

I have prayed to understand God's plan for the destiny of my daughter and have spoken this into her life. I have prayed to walk in righteousness that I might leave footprints for my child to follow that will empower her to become all that God has designed her to be in life.

Whose Mind?

At some point you will find yourself in a predicament where you have to make a decision whether to say yes or no. Rather than beating around the bush, I will tell you right away that I'm talking about sex. There, I said it. Now let's talk about it.

The world we live in right now has given us the green light to get involved sexually with no limitations. In fact, these days, you are considered very "uncool" or a nerd or something similar if you don't. It has gotten too easy, these days, to forget who we really are. We have forgotten that we are children of the Living God whose commandments don't change with the times. Ask yourself the question, "Am I doing what others are doing because it's the right thing, or do I feel pressured by my peers or a boyfriend?"

When I was growing up, my dad had a saying in our house that almost became a mantra, "Have your own mind." He drilled that into me and my siblings until we heard it in our sleep. It made a difference, but I would like to go one better than my Dad and remind us that we need to *have the mind of Christ* (I Cor. 2:16). That simply means to follow God's way. In other words, try to live life based on His Word – not just follow our own ideas.

There will be many opportunities to do the wrong thing, but remembering to have the mind of Christ will give you the courage to do the right thing, the godly thing. The good news is that if you have already crossed that line, it's **never too late** to get back on the right track. Keeping your relationship with God in the forefront of your mind will allow the Holy Spirit to speak to your heart and guide you down a path that leads to a life of blessings.

Fit for the Ride of Your Life

Your body was designed to last a lifetime. How you treat it will determine the length and quality of your life. Love your body. The genes that came together to create you are unique and God given. Your body was put together to work perfectly, and that happens best when it is healthy. Give it nutritious food, ample water, consistent exercise and gentle kindness. Pouring excessive fat, sugar and caffeine into your body will keep it from working at its best. To feel good and be fit, eat lots of fruit, vegetables, whole grains, protein and good carbohydrates.

Don't smoke. You will considerably decrease your chances of getting heart disease, cancer, high blood pressure and diabetes. Avoid alcohol. If you partake, always do it in moderation and never drink and drive. Also, remember to incorporate 20 minutes of exercise into each day – or an hour three days a week. Go for a walk at the mall. Rollerblade with a friend. Ride a bike or join an exercise class. Treat your body with respect. Don't hold it to impossible standards. Over-exercising can cause lasting injuries.

Healthy living means keeping your mind healthy. Learn how to deal with stress. Let the little stuff go. Life is meant to be savored. Remember, each day your life starts anew. Don't drag old worries and wounds along. Be happy. Be at peace. Forgive. Embrace the joy in life. Get plenty of rest. It will increase your energy, resistance to illness and ability to concentrate. Make the bedroom a place of refuge where you read, listen to music and rest.

Know your body. Learn how to do a breast self-exam. Check your skin regularly for unusual lumps or moles. If something doesn't seem right, check it out. You know your body better than anyone. Listen to it. Respect it. Love it.

Eighth Grade Wisdom

Be cool. Stay sweet, and don't change for anyone. These simple words donned the covers of eighth grade yearbooks at Taft Jr. High. While cliché and admittedly corny, these words have come to life in a way that I never expected. Had I any idea about the twists and turns that would become my life's story, I would have paid more attention to those simple words with such a profound message.

Yes, I would have methodically, with calculated precision, etched those simple words on the tablet of my heart – taking care to spell each word correctly, using proper spacing, punctuating with feeling and purpose.

I would capitalize the "B" in "be cool" focusing on the difference between who you are and how you behave. To "be" is a constant state that doesn't waiver from minutes to hours or days – to *be* calm, collected and rational. To truly *be* cool is a **decision** you make about how you will handle life's challenges throughout the years to come.

I would underline the "<u>stay</u>" in "stay sweet", realizing that I was born that way – sweet, looking at life through the purest of lenses, not yet knowing the dangers or heartache that lie ahead in such a world as this.

In all capital letters I would write "DON'T CHANGE FOR ANYONE". This is not a suggestion; it's a mandate – a call to action, a pleading request.

I want you to understand that the hard balls life throws at you will offer you suggestions about the way you relate to people, the world and even yourself. God designed you himself – the rough places and jagged edges. Even those slight irregularities and misplaced discolorations have a purpose. They make up the perfectly imperfect you.

So let God change you, not people, circumstances or life. You are truly one of a kind. Stand out! Be exactly who you were meant to be. You'll be great at it!

Allonna J. Stovall

Stop! Drop! and Roll!

While going through one of the most difficult times in my life, I remember waking up in the middle of the night with these resounding words in my spirit: STOP, DROP, and ROLL. I immediately knew that the Lord was communicating something very strategic to me, so I began to reflect on these words.

The first thing that came to me was the memory of an elementary school teacher giving us instructions in case of a fire. She said we should STOP the panic or fear. Now that is exactly what Jesus said to the disciples that found themselves in the middle of a storm while at sea, "Fear Not." II Timothy 1:7 says, "God has not given us a spirit of fear, but of power, and of love, and of a sound mind." (NKJV)

The second thing my teacher said was to, "DROP to your knees." She explained that we should stay down as low as possible since that was where our source of oxygen was. I immediately saw the spiritual parallel of prayer. As I pondered prayer's power, I could hear the words of the old-timers saying "pray 'til you pray through" meaning pray until you have peace. The understanding of those words filled my heart as the revelation became so clear from Romans 16:20: "and the God of Peace shall soon crush Satan under your feet." (NKJV) What words of wisdom to me at that moment! With the peace of God flooding my heart, I knew that I was ready to move forward.

My teacher further explained that after you stop and drop, you should be able to ROLL. What an excitement filled my heart as I realized that the fear of my circumstances had gone and that God had given me the power to roll right through my greatest challenge into victory. "Let the peace of God rule in your hearts." (Colossians 3:15, NKJV)

Pastor Reneé Clark

Our Authors

Thira Simon, a native of Beaumont, Texas, is a mother of two with a Bachelor of Arts in Theology. She is an entrepreneur and Certified Faith-Based Counselor. Besides leading the Single's Ministry at Triumph Church in Beaumont, she inspires others as a powerful public speaker.

Pat Avery has broken glass ceilings as a woman and as a minority in Southeast Texas industry. The Beaumont Chamber awarded her the prestigious "Athena Award" in 2009. Many nonprofits in the area – from arts to education to industrial organizations – benefit from her passion to serve the community.

Shari Griffin is the mother of a daughter, a son, and a new daughter-in-law, all in their twenties. She has been married to her husband, John, for almost 30 years. They live in Beaumont, Texas, where Shari is a private music teacher and coordinates church children's choirs.

Pamela A. Stovall co-authored the book, *Marriage is Not for the Faint of Heart* with husband, Adrian, in 2005. They currently serve as pastors and marriage coaches at Triumph Church in Beaumont, Texas. Pamela holds a position on the Board of Directors for Empowering Women as Leaders (EWL). She is the mother of three adult children and grandmother of ten.

Joy Crenshaw is a devoted wife, mother of four, and grandmother of seven. She has served on Beaumont's Young Life board 25 years. She also serves on Family Services board and Lamar University Fine Arts advisory board. She is very active in First United Methodist Church, including teaching Sunday School classes for five-year-olds.

Beth Middleton is a mother of 4 with her husband of 17 years. She has worked as a Corporate Trainer and is currently an Adjunct Professor. Beth recently completed an L.L.M. (Master of Laws) and is now a candidate for a J.S.D. (Doctor of the Science of Law). In her spare time, she is an aspiring author of academic textbooks and motivational writings.

Mary Ann Reid is the daughter of W. B. and Doris Goudeau, wife to Robert, and mother to Chelsea, Kyle, Reece and Jessica. She is currently the President of the Greater Port Arthur Chamber of Commerce and has a background in community relations. She is happy with her life.

Karen L. Bates is an ordained Minister and has pastored for more than 10 years. She is also a singer, a writer and an editor. She earned a Master's degree from Asbury Theological Seminary and completed her undergraduate work at Wilberforce University. She currently lives in Maryland.

Linda Combs Sculley is a credentialed Minister with Assemblies of God, works as a consultant with RESULTS 4 Nonprofits, and serves as a chaplain to local corporations. She founded Christian Women's Job Corps - Golden Triangle. She and her husband Mike have five adult children and worship at Cathedral in the Pines.

Verna Rutherford is a native of Port Arthur, Texas, having a long history of leadership and community service in Southeast Texas. Her professional and personal background includes government and public affairs, community and economic development, along with being an entrepreneur and community volunteer.

Ivy Stegall is a graduate of the University of Northern Iowa with a Bachelor of Arts in education. After a successful elementary school career, Ivy made the decision to be a stay-at-home mom and home school her two little girls – a decision she does not regret in the least.

April K. Tyler holds a Bachelor's of Business Administration from Iowa State University. She is a wife and, currently, stay-at-home mom. Prior to motherhood, April was the assistant editor for the magazine, *Pathway*, published by The Church on the Way and project manager for Foursquare Communications. She and her family reside in Southern California.

Pastor Lindsay Clark captured the Mrs. Texas title in 2009. Lindsay and her husband, Randon have 2 children, and are both ordained Ministers who jointly lead the pastoral team at Triumph Church in Beaumont, Texas. She also holds a board position with the nonprofit organization, Empowering Women as Leaders.

Carolyn Pineda is an experienced business leader with more than 20 years in corporate America with Fortune 500 companies. In addition to experience in the corporate world, Carolyn is the founder of a nonprofit, Empowering Woman as Leaders. She has also provided consulting services to nonprofits.

Gail Cawley Showalter is a native of Southeast Texas, a mother of three, step-mom of three more, and Nana to a dozen. She taught children with visual impairments for eight years, and since 1998, has worked as a certified personality specialist, writer, and speaker. In 2006 she founded Single Moms, Overjoyed, Rejuvenated, and Empowered (SMORE)! Gail is a published author and has presented workshops throughout the United States.

Elaine Allums was appointed to the Kountze City Council in 1999 and has been Mayor Pro Tem for the City of Kountze, Texas for the last ten years. She is Vice-President of the Kountze Economic Development Corporation and is also on the boards of many vital organizations. Elaine and husband, Donald, have two daughters.

Cherie H. Gall is an attorney and born-again believer living in Athens, Ohio with her pastor/attorney husband and their teenage daughter. She and her husband have been married for over 27 years and are partners in a law firm. Her husband is pastor of Abundant Life Church, a Spirit-filled, Word of Faith Church.

Marilyn Smith has 29 years of experience in Workforce. Reared by a strong mother and older sister, Jackie, her family was financially poor, but spiritually rich. She has a Bachelors of Social Work degree from Lamar University. She and her siblings remain avid readers. She is married and has two children.

Karen Bourdier's career at a Fortune 500 company has involved her in serving communities and nonprofits in the southeast Texas region. Her focus has been on economic development, workforce, leadership, and diversity. She and her husband worship and are actively involved at Triumph Church - Beaumont campus.

Becky Ames is the Executive Director of the Atria Collier Park Retirement and Assisted Living Community and was elected as Mayor in 2007 to the City of Beaumont, Texas in the Southeast Texas region. At the time of this printing, she is currently serving in both roles.

Based in Hedrick, Iowa, **Sharon Benell** has been a preacher of the Gospel of Jesus Christ around the world for over thirty years. She is also an anointed singer and typically ministers in music prior to preaching or teaching. She and her husband, Gary, have been married 48 years at the time of this printing, having raised three children and ten foster girls.

In her career in higher education, **Yolanda Avery** has guided over 10,000 students in employment preparation and career services in the workforce. She volunteers for numerous nonprofits and organizations in the region. Her husband and two boys worship with her at Mt. Gilead Missionary Baptist Church in Beaumont, Texas where she is involved with the youth and is the praise dance leader.

Waldine Small is an ordained Minister and has a Master's Degree in Scriptural Psychology. Through her profession as Faith-Based Counselor and LCDC, she helps restore people to a healthy relationship with God, family and community. She is happily married to Elton 40 years; proud mother of one daughter and a precious grandson.

Jane McBride is an award-winning journalist, blogger, author and outspoken advocate who has tackled domestic abuse, child abuse, child pornography and breast cancer awareness during 18 years as a columnist for the Beaumont Enterprise. Jane holds the Hearst Corporation's Eagle Award. Her book "Grace, Gratitude & Generosity," was published Nov. 2009.

Allonna Stovall resides in Des Moines, Iowa where she is a full-time homemaker raising six children (ages 2, 3, 4, 6, 7, and 8) with her husband of eleven years, Damien. A 1999 graduate of the University of Northern Iowa, she teaches water aerobics at the local YMCA, hosts children's book clubs, does personal shopping and has served as a youth minister for the past 11 years at her church.

Pastor Reneé Clark is an ordained Minister who travels extensively as a conference and camp meeting speaker while serving as a founding pastor of Triumph Church with her husband Randy. She is wonderfully gifted in music and the arts and carries a powerful revivalist anointing that ignites the purposes and destiny of God in the hearts of the people.

Who's In the Photographs?

Acknowledgements

To our authors - Thank you for sharing openly and honestly the messages from your life experiences so important for our next generation of young Christian women.

To our models - Thank you for portraying caring, honest, and open communication between women of two generations through your facial expressions, eye contact, and body language. You provide a visual example to many mothers and daughters of how to communicate.

To our reviewers - Thank you for your encouraging words and affirmations.

To our proofer - Thanks for lending another set of eyes to the details of spelling, punctuation, and grammar. After all, we need to set a good example for the young ladies reading this book about the importance of all those details and the importance of doing everything with excellence.

To our husbands, Adrian and Terry – Without your support and encouragement, we would have fallen far short of our goal. Thank you. What blessings you are!

To everyone who had even the smallest part in making this book possible – Thank you from the bottom of our hearts.

www.ingramcontent.com/pod-product-compliance
Lightning Source LLC
Chambersburg PA
CBRC091800090426
42811CB00021B/1899